Contents

Where is space? 4

Sunny days 6

The Moon 8

Amazing planets 10

Endless stars 12

Blast off! 14

Inside a spacecraft 16

On the Moon 18

Exploring Mars 20

Quiz 22

Glossary and answers 23

Index 24

Words in **bold** are in the glossary on page 23.

Where is space?

We live on a round, rocky **planet** called the Earth. A thin blanket of air surrounds the Earth. Space begins where the air ends.

Space includes the Sun, the Moon and the stars.

When you look into a clear sky you are looking into space.

The Earth is a planet in space. The Sun, the Moon and the stars are all in space, too.

Sunny days

The Earth spins around in space. The Sun lights up the side of the Earth that faces it.

The Sun is a huge, burning ball of **gas** in space. It is so bright and hot that its light and warmth reach us here on the Earth.

The Earth spins around on an imaginary line, called its **axis**. It takes 24 hours to make one spin. Half of the Earth is in sunlight at any time. The rest is dark. This gives us day and night.

Axis

7

The Moon

The Moon travels around the Earth. It takes about 27 days for the Moon to go all the way around the Earth.

We see the Moon because the Sun shines on it. Every month the part of the Moon we see slowly changes from a full circle to a slim crescent, then back to a full circle.

**The Moon goes around the Earth.
It is lit by the Sun.**

Amazing planets

The Sun is at the centre of the **Solar System**. The Solar System has eight planets, including Jupiter, the biggest planet.

The planets in the Solar System, including the Earth, **orbit** the Sun. This means that each moves in its own huge circle around the Sun.

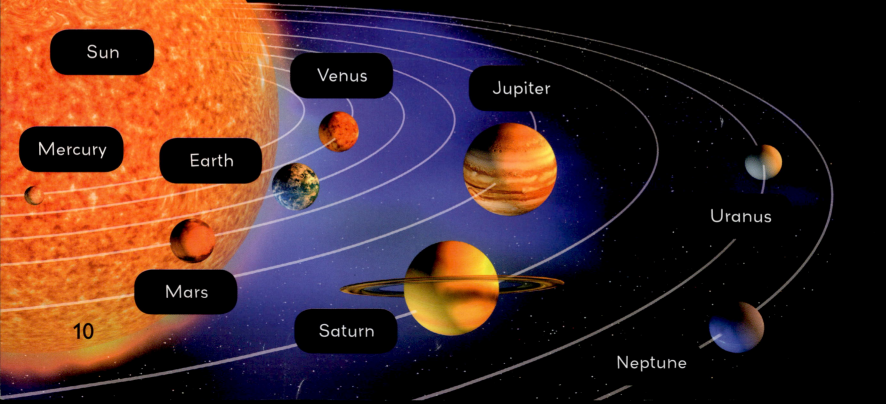

Sun

Mercury

Earth

Venus

Jupiter

Mars

Saturn

Uranus

Neptune

The Earth and seven other planets move around the Sun. Jupiter is the biggest planet.

Endless stars

Stars are
very far away.
We see them as
tiny lights in
the night
sky.

Stars twinkle
in the night sky.
Each star is a
burning ball
of gas, like the
Sun. Stars
are so far
away that we
see them as
tiny lights.

Some of the
brightest stars
form shapes
in the sky. This
group of stars
is called Orion.

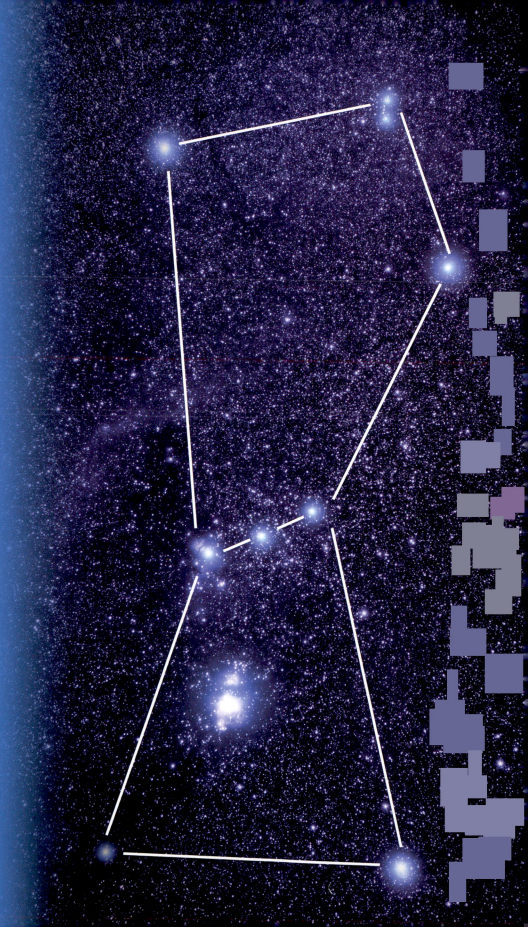

Blast off!

Astronauts travel into space in a **spacecraft**. A huge **rocket** lifts the spacecraft up through the air.

Then the rocket falls back to the Earth. The spacecraft travels on into space.

A spacecraft takes astronauts into space. A rocket lifts the spacecraft high into the air.

Inside a spacecraft

There is no air in space. A spacecraft takes its own air into space so that astronauts can breathe.

On the Earth, **gravity** pulls things to the ground. In space, gravity is less strong. Everything in a spacecraft floats, even food!

Gravity is less strong in space. Everything floats there!

17

On the Moon

More than 40 years ago, astronauts walked on the Moon. They raised a flag and brought back some Moon rocks to the Earth for scientists to study.

The Moon has no air, so the astronauts wore **spacesuits** when they were outside the spacecraft. The spacesuits protected the astronauts and gave them air to breathe.

Astronauts walked on the Moon. They wore spacesuits to keep them safe.

Exploring Mars

Mars is much further away from the Earth than the Moon. Mars is sometimes called the Red Planet because its rocks are red.

Scientists use **robots** to explore Mars. The robots send information back to the Earth. Astronauts hope to visit Mars one day.

Mars is a long
way from the
Earth. We use robots
to find out about it.

Quiz

1. What is the Moon lit by?

2. Which is the biggest planet in the Solar System?

3. Why does food float in space?

4. What did astronauts raise on the Moon?

Glossary

astronaut a person who travels into space

axis an imaginary line from the North Pole to the South Pole through the centre of the Earth

gas a substance that is neither solid nor liquid and is able to float in air. We cannot usually see gases

gravity a force that pulls one object towards another

orbit move round and round an object in space

planet a large object in space that orbits the Sun

robot a machine that works by itself

rocket an engine that blasts things into space

Solar System the Sun and all the objects that orbit it, including the planets

spacecraft a vehicle that travels into space

spacesuit a special suit that keeps an astronaut alive in space outside a spacecraft

Answers to the quiz:
1. The Sun.
2. Jupiter.
3. Because gravity is less strong there.
4. A flag.

23

Index

air 4, 16, 19
astronauts 14, 15, 16, 18, 19, 20

Earth, the 4, 5, 6, 7, 8, 9, 10, 11, 14, 16, 18, 20, 21
  axis 7

gravity 16, 17

Mars 20–21
Moon, the 4, 5, 8–9, 18–19
  rocks 19

Orion 13

robots 20–21
rockets 14, 15

Solar System, the 10–11
spacecrafts 14, 15, 16
spacesuits 19
stars 12–13
Sun, the 4, 5, 6–7

Franklin Watts
Published in Great Britain in 2017 by
The Watts Publishing Group

Copyright ©The Watts Publishing
Group 2015

All rights reserved.

Series Editor: Julia Bird
Series Advisor: Karina Law
Series Design: Basement68

Dewey number: 629.4
ISBN 978 1 4451 3810 7

Every attempt has been made to clear
copyright. Should there be any
inadvertent omission please apply to
the publisher for rectification.

Picture credits: Bettmann/Corbis: 15. Steve Biegler/Shutterstock: 9, 22tl.
Marcel Clemens/Nasa/Shutterstock: 3c, 11, 22tr. Igor Dabari/Shutterstock: 13.
s decoret/Dreamstime: front cover. Mark M Lawrence/Corbis: 14.
S R Lee PhotoTravellers/Shutterstock: 6. Walter Myers/Alamy: 20.
NASA: 2, 3b, 16, 17, 18, 21, 22bl, 22br. S Nike/Shutterstock: 12.
Orla/Shutterstock: 10. paffy/Shutterstock: 5. siraphat/Shutterstock: 19, 23.
somartin/Shutterstock: 4. Andrzej Wojcicki/SPL/Alamy: 1, 7.
Yarygin/Shutterstock: 3t, 8.

Printed in China

Franklin Watts
An imprint of
Hachette Children's Group
Part of The Watts Publishing Group
Carmelite House
50 Victoria Embankment
London EC4Y 0DZ

An Hachette UK Company

www.hachette.co.uk
www.franklinwatts.co.uk